Lovin' Each Day

Unleash Your Passions for a Life of
Love, Health, and Happiness

Lovin' Each Day

Unleash Your Passions for a Life of Love, Health, and Happiness

By Mike Smith

ISBN: 978-1-945446-03-0

YouSpeakIt
PUBLISHING
The Easy Way
to Get Your Book
Done Right™

www.YouSpeakItPublishing.com

Dedication

Always to Erika. You are my forever-crazy-love and the inspiration for everything I ever do in this life.

Acknowledgments

Thank you to my six beautiful kids: Brice, Eliana, Cooper, Eva, Abby, and Dylan.

Thank you to Angela Schoonhoven and Bob Schoonhoven.

Thank you to Earlene Smith.

Thank you Marty Tomao; Kevin Roof; Codey Brown; King Tech; Sway Calloway; Kxng Crooked; Jonathan Hay; Michael Kelly; my dad, Jack Smith; Bella; Tim Gorman; Kim Bailey Shouse; Christina Bear; Kat Atwood; and Wayne Halper.

Contents

Introduction

Are you ready to shake off all of the feelings of mediocrity?

Are you finished living a life of quiet desperation?

Are you looking for a mid-life renaissance in your personal life and career?

Are you looking for a way to build a life path filled with joy?

If your answer to any of these questions is yes, this is the book you need to read. I'm not saying that by reading this book your life is going to be transformed. What I am saying is that you're reading a book about someone whose life was transformed.

Whatever your current state of life, if you picked up this book, you are definitely feeling that something is missing from your life, whether it be in your career, your personal life, or both. This book can be a road map for you, showing you how to take a critical look at yourself and where you are today, and giving you some tools and insights that you can use to give yourself a better tomorrow.

In this book you will read about my journey. You will read about my path to a joyful and fulfilling life. You will have the opportunity to see what I discovered through trial and error about making positive changes to improve my physical, emotional, and spiritual health, and to build a remarkably happy personal life and successful career.

I wrote this book because I have experienced a unique journey that is worthwhile to share. Ten years ago, my life was not happy. I had a failed business; I was in a marriage that I was not happy with. I was feeling extremely unfulfilled. I was overweight and was not satisfied with my appearance.

Today, I am in great shape, I am a successful singer-songwriter who stars on a major TV show, I am married to the girl I never stopped loving, and I am living out my childhood fantasy every day. I don't come from money, and I am no different than anyone else. If I can change my life, so can you.

It all started with a dream I had one day. I was lying on the floor watching TV, and I fell asleep. I had a dream that there was a calendar next to my television, and the days started blowing off the calendar outside. All of a sudden, it was 2070, and I was ninety years old. I looked up and was in the exact same position that I had been in sixty years earlier.

I woke up from that dream in a cold sweat and said to myself: *I can't believe that this is all my life is cracked up to be.*

I made a decision at that moment that I was going to change my life.

I started by getting myself in shape. The next step was to reintroduce myself to my passions, which for me were centered on music. Then I made a hard, critical assessment of my personal life. Finally, I went where everybody told me I was a fool to go.

The best way to read this book is not to look at it as a workbook, but to read my story and relate it to your own circumstances. Use my life as an example of how to effect change; apply my tools to your own circumstances. Take the elements that apply to you and use them where they can help you on your own unique life path.

Your life may be very different from mine. You might be happy with how you are physically, you could be very happy in your marriage, or you could be very happy in your career. This book is not meant to tell you what you should do; it is meant to give you some understanding of the different elements in life that affect you. It is meant to inspire you to seek out your best self and your best life possible.

What I hope everybody gains from reading this book is the importance of living a life with passion. Don't just *exist*, but *live*.

Benjamin Franklin said, "Most people die when they're twenty-five, but they don't have their funeral until they are seventy-five."

When I look at some of the people around me, I think that can be very true.

As you observe most of your friends and family, how many of them talk about the good old days?

They talk about high school and college and all these days when they felt young and are living in the past.

It is never too late. You have the right to feel alive every day. Be alive and pursue what you love.

CHAPTER ONE

Health

Before you can fully address how you feel about your life, career, marriage, or other issues, you should first assess your personal health.

How do you feel?

What health issues do you need to improve?

There are three main components to consider, and they are all equally important:

- Your diet: What are you putting into your body?

- Your level of exercise: How are you moving your body?

- Your inner state: How is your mental and emotional well-being?

This chapter explores these elements in detail.

DIET

If you are feeling unhealthy in any way, shape, or form, you should first look at your diet. In the United States and perhaps, in the world in general, everybody wants to overmedicate all of their issues and try to pop a pill to correct whatever they are feeling.

I am a firm believer that the best medicine for your body is what you eat and drink. For health and well-being in the long term, good nutrition is vital.

I have spent a lot of time testing my own body to figure out what foods and drinks work for me and what don't work for me; not only relative to weight loss, but to my overall health as well.

My Weight-Loss Journey

In 2002, I quit smoking and, as is common, I gained weight. I put on twenty pounds. Six years later, I still carried it with me. I had a hard time losing weight primarily because I had a horrible diet. I had never lost the bad habits of youth — eating food like cheeseburgers nearly every day.

In March of 2008, I had major stomach issues with a great deal of pain. I went to a doctor who wanted to put me on steroids and I faced the choice:

Do I want to start going down the road of having all of these crazy medicines put in me and risking all of the potential side effects?

Or did I want to find an alternative route to fix my issues with my stomach?

I did some research and discovered that I did not have enough fiber in my diet. What I was eating was terrible. I was shocked that the doctor did not figure this out.

I started to change my diet on my own. At this point I was just experimenting with whether I could alter my symptoms simply by changing my diet. Before you do anything I describe here, please consult with your healthcare provider.

First, I began taking a high-fiber supplement containing psyllium husk and within five days, my stomach pain was completely gone.

Second, I decided to cleanse my body by not eating any red meat for fifteen days. I ate egg noodles, brown rice, eggs, wheat toast, and things like that for about fifteen days. I ended up dropping about fifteen pounds.

Right after that, I reversed my approach and ate only high-protein foods. I lost another fifteen pounds in two weeks. I went from almost all non-fat to almost all fat and protein. It was an interesting change, and it worked.

I continued to investigate the effect of different foods on my body. Over time, I have found a balance that works for me. For the last seven years, I haven't been eating carbs on Mondays and Tuesdays. Wednesdays, I have a cheat day and eat whatever I want. Thursdays, Fridays, and Saturdays, I eat very little carbs, and Sundays, I have another cheat day and eat whatever I want. This pattern has worked well for me.

Crafting Your Own Personalized Diet

Part of my experimentation and analysis was to get on a scale every morning and figure out what foods were working for me and what wasn't working for me. I experimented with different categories of food, eating certain things consistently on a given day. The next morning, I would weigh in and figure out what the effect was.

In this way, I figured out what foods I lost weight on and what I gained weight on. I kept track of this through a food journal and through this analysis I was able to determine my own best diet.

Essentially, what I ended up choosing were basic foods I could eat day in and day out.

This strategy may not work exactly the same for everyone. For example, compared to a man, a woman's weight can fluctuate a great deal with hormonal changes. When my wife tried to experiment with her diet, she had to account for her cycle fluctuations in order to do this kind of analysis.

But for me, certain foods emerged from my experiments as my friends. Eggs, steak, chicken, brown rice, salad, all kinds of veggies, and even baked potatoes were all great for me. Veggie chili worked, too. The foods that put weight on me were processed foods, such as white rice and pizza, and this was very obvious.

But the other thing that was very interesting to me was that having those two cheat days a week—Wednesday and Sunday—actually accelerated my metabolism. I would see a weight gain the next morning, but I would drop more weight two days later than the day before my cheat day. The cheat days seemed important to *trick* my metabolism, keeping my metabolism from slowing down in order to conserve weight.

As I experimented, I discovered the foods that helped me lose weight and made me feel good.

How can you craft your own personalized diet?

Below is a summary of my general strategy:

- Create a food journal.
- Every day, write down what you eat.
- Write down how you feel after eating.
- Weigh yourself each morning.
- Keep a list of the foods that make you gain weight.
- Keep a list of the foods that result in weight loss.

- When you have enough data, design a diet of foods that you like, that make you feel good, and that bring you closer to your weight goals.

You are likely to find, like I did, that highly processed foods contribute to weight gain. If you are trying to lose weight, be sure to take a good look at the processed foods in your diet.

Which foods make your body feel best?

You may decide to eat organic foods. You may adopt a vegetarian diet or opt for a high-meat diet. You must make your own choices; choose whatever works best for you and your body as well as your spirituality. The important part is that you really analyze what you are putting in your body, figure out how different foods affect you, and choose foods that enhance your health and well-being.

Maintaining Weight for the Long-Term

It is notoriously difficult to maintain weight once you've reached a weight-loss goal. And whether or not you have a weight struggle, once you have established a healthy diet, it can be difficult to maintain that diet over the long term.

If you are using an approach like mine, the key to maintain it long term is *never to feel guilty about your cheat days*.

Each week, if you can focus the fact that you only have to have two or three days where you have to eat super healthy before a day when you can eat anything you want, you will have more chance of success.

This is how I have been able to keep my weight off for the past seven years; I'm never looking at my diet plan in more than three-day increments at a time.

Here are the key points of my approach for the long-term:

- Make a weekly plan based on your food journal.

- Incorporate *cheat* days into your diet program and don't feel guilty about them.

- Choose foods that you like to eat; don't design a diet of foods you despise.

- Eat *real* food.

- Don't bother with protein shakes.

- Don't use diet supplements.

- If you are trying to lose weight, wait until you reach your target weight before you start a serious exercise regimen.

Below is an example of my diet week. I am a creature of habit, so I will eat from the same choices often.

On Mondays and Tuesdays, this selection keeps me super satisfied:

For breakfast, I'll have three eggs and two pieces of high-fiber, whole-wheat toast.

For lunch, my selections vary more than other meals — a peanut butter and jelly sandwich with high-fiber, whole-wheat bread, or a baked potato with veggie chili, or Mexican food, or sushi.

For an afternoon snack, I eat pumpkin seeds.

For dinner, I have a bone-in rib eye and a salad.

On Wednesday, I will eat whatever I want — you'll notice that these are foods that most dieters normally would try to avoid:

- For breakfast, I often eat pancakes.
- For lunch, I'll have a cheeseburger and French fries.
- For a snack, I'll have pretzels or chips.
- Dinner could be pizza.

On Thursday, Friday, and Saturday, I go back to a Monday-and-Tuesday selection.

On Sunday, I eat whatever I want.

I have maintained my body weight within five pounds for seven years. It's pretty cool how well this plan has worked for so many years. Currently, I also have an intense workout schedule and we'll talk about exercise in the next section. But as I've already stated, it's best if you don't start exercising before achieving your desired weight. You want to lose the weight first. That is key.

EXERCISE

Why should you wait to incorporate exercise?

The first step is to lose weight and get on a healthy diet. Note that when I say *diet*, I'm not talking about getting on a diet to lose weight. I'm talking about your overall physical nutrition. First, you want to select items for your healthy diet and you want to get to your target weight prior to exercising.

Why should you wait until you get to your target weight?

You might be thinking that you'll lose weight faster if you exercise at the same time you are dieting. That sounds logical, but if you start an exercise regimen at the same time you are trying to lose weight, you will make yourself extra hungry, and risk stalling your weight loss. Lose the weight first, and once you are at the weight you want to be, it is time to start exercising.

My Exercise Regimen

I'm a bit of an extremist and this kind of regimen may not be right for you, but this is what I do every day. My daily regimen is two hundred push-ups a day. I do one hundred incline push-ups and then one hundred regular push-ups. In addition to that, I either run or lift weights five out of seven days a week.

The key is to be *always doing something*, but in addition, it is a combination of the quick bursts of strength training and long-term endurance training that is most effective. You also need to take into account what else you are actually doing in that given day.

For example, on Mondays and Tuesdays I typically don't run because I am not eating that many carbs. On those days I tend to focus on strength training, three or four out of those five days. If I am not eating quite as many carbs, I don't have to burn as many calories, so running isn't as important.

On my cheat days, I will typically go on a long run because what I'm eating on my cheat days gets offset by the running.

When you exercise, the key is making sure that you are using the fuel you are putting in your body. If you are eating carbs, you run to burn it off. If you are having a day of no carbs and lots of protein, then strength training is important for building muscle, which uses the protein.

Think about what you want to do to sculpt your body:

Are you looking to bulk up or just to add some lean muscular lines?

Depending on what you're looking to accomplish, you can do more repetitions with low weights to go for lean lines, or a bit heavier weights with fewer repetitions if you want to be bulkier. That is a personal choice.

The key is to work out for at least thirty minutes for five of the seven days in a week and rotate what you are doing so you give yourself time to rest. I always try to take two days of rest from anything during a week let my body repair. That is very important.

To summarize:

- Work out at least thirty minutes for five days each week.

- Do both quick burst exercise and endurance activities.

- Focus on calorie burning activities on high-carb days.

- Lift weights for body sculpting.

- Focus on strength training exercise on high protein days.

- Rotate activities and incorporate rest days.

How You Can Start

Be careful about the goals you set. They can make all the difference.

The way to get started is to start small. Start with push-ups every day. Do as many as you can each day. The next day, add one more to the number you did the day before.

The key to all of this is setting small parameters.

Don't think: *I have to do two hundred push-ups starting today.*

Make your goals small enough so they are achievable. Follow the same strategies as the dieting we talked about, in which you only have to go two days and then can eat whatever you want. Keeping goals small but consistent will keep you on track.

When you break things down in smaller components and stick to them over the course of a year, you will have completely changed who you are two days at a time.

So start with ten push-ups, then go to eleven the next day. In ninety days, you will be at one hundred push-ups. In only three months, you're there!

The same thing can be applied to running. When I started running, I ran as far as I could without stopping, and it was pathetic. I could only go for ten minutes; it was horrible. But instead of giving up, I made a goal to add one minute every day until I got to forty minutes.

It took me a month to run that time nonstop, and I was running as slowly as a human being could possibly run without it actually being called walking.

But I did it!

I got to forty minutes. Even though it may have taken me longer to run a mile than it would have to walk a mile, I reached my goal.

Now, I can run a 10K — six and a half miles — in under fifty minutes. When I first started, I was running two miles in forty minutes.

The idea is making *incremental changes*.

Before you know it, you will look back and say, "Holy cow, I can't believe I accomplished that!"

How to Reach Your Long-Term Goals

What are your long-term goals?

Mine were to get healthy, lose weight, and feel great.

It took me at least a year to get to a state of maintenance. Between eating and exercise, I figured out the mechanics for staying healthy and maintaining my weight. Once you get this figured out for yourself, you will be in the zone to maintain and can set some new goals.

Once you are at this state:

- Weigh yourself every morning.

- Keep a five-pound threshold in mind.

- If you get to the high side of the threshold, cut back on carbs and increase exercise.

- If you get to the low side of the threshold, you can go easier on exercise.

- It's all right to give yourself extra cheat days occasionally when your weight is low.

- Don't go outside your five-pound range, neither under nor over.

OVERALL EMOTIONAL WELL-BEING

As I stated at the beginning of this chapter, there are three components to healthy living:

1. Make sure what you are putting inside of your body is maintaining your health.

2. Make sure that you are moving your body and keeping it healthy.

3. Make sure you are noticing your mental and emotional well-being.

I want to repeat this third point because it does not get a lot of attention: in order for you to stay in balance, you need to be healthy emotionally.

My Emotional Journey

In 2008, I should have been a happy person. My financial situation had improved greatly, dramatically rebounding after a business failure five years earlier. I had all the money I needed, I had two beautiful healthy intelligent children, and I was in what most people would perceive as a good marriage.

Life should have been good. The truth was, I was tragically unhappy.

I was absolutely miserable every day. The worst day of my life was the day I sold my businesses for a sizable amount of money. It was when I considered all the free time I had just gained that I realized how truly unhappy I was with my life.

Why was I so unhappy?

Because I felt completely unfulfilled.

At this time, because of the stomach issues I was having, I opted to make some changes. I realized that I had transferred my compulsion to smoke into a compulsion to eat. I was blocking my feelings and emotions by eating to avoid dealing with what I was feeling.

When I changed how I ate, I no longer had the emotional crutch I was relying on to block out my feelings.

Without the crutch, I truly started feeling again, and the feelings hit me like a ton of bricks.

I felt very sad, and I was overwhelmed by a feeling of emptiness. I had always been a very happy person. I was not equipped to deal with feeling this kind of sadness for an extended period.

It was at this moment I discovered two things I hadn't wanted to admit:

1. I had squandered my musical talents and gifts and was not pursuing the career I wanted.

2. I was not in love with my wife.

Music and Love

I have played the guitar since before I was in kindergarten. I now play twelve instruments and since 2008, I have probably written over five thousand songs. However, there was a ten-year period before 2008 during which all of these skills lay dormant. I barely played my guitar; I wrote very rarely. I had set aside a big part of who I was.

It was in this moment of profound despair that I rediscovered my guitar and my ability to write songs. What I found shocked and amazed me at the same time.

I discovered that my ability to understand my emotions was directly connected to my songwriting— writing is how I process what I feel. I would come up with a melody and start singing lyrics as a stream of consciousness. When I'd review what I had written during the creative process, it would express exactly what I was feeling.

The songs that started coming out of me at first were somewhat remedial, but the messages were poignant and clear. I was writing about being lonely, sad, and unfulfilled. The fact that I was in a loveless marriage was undeniable.

To put this in context, I need to tell you about Erika. Erika was my college girlfriend. She was the most incredible person I had ever met. Stunningly beautiful, wildly talented, she was an accomplished ballerina and modern dancer by the age of seventeen. She was intelligent, funny, sincere, and sweet.

The first moment I laid eyes on her, I walked over to her and told her that someday we would be together, and then I walked away. I was right. Several weeks later we started accidentally running into each other everywhere. Soon after that, we were a couple.

Our relationship was the most electric, passionate, and the deepest connection I have ever felt in my life. We became attached to each other and shut out the rest of the world. We got engaged and almost married.

However, with all of that passion came a lot of fear and emotion that Erika and I weren't equipped to handle. We both came from very difficult childhoods. We both brought to our relationship a lot of emotional baggage. After dating for three years, we broke up.

I say all of this to explain more about my state of being in 2008. I hadn't seen or heard from Erika for ten years, and I had been with my first wife, Alison, for most of the time after Erika and I broke up. Alison and I had a friendly relationship. There was nothing dark or bad in our relationship. We got along fine, and we could be in the same house together without driving each other crazy.

However, I had no idea how much I missed feeling passion for someone until I started having all of this emotion pour out through my music.

Now in fairness, Alison and I were having an extended rocky road after the birth of our second child. We were arguing a lot. It seemed what we each wanted out of life had grown and changed. She was perfectly content with a simple life, and I apparently was not. It led to a lot of discontent between us. She kept trying to fix our marriage, but I soon realized how deeply disconnected I was.

After struggling with this for over a year, I decided to take a leap into the unknown and I left Alison.

What happened after that was truly the most remarkable thing that has happened to me.

On the tenth anniversary of our breakup, Erika and I reconnected when she added me as a friend on Facebook. When I told her she had done this on the anniversary of our breakup, she was surprised; it was unintentional. She was living three hours away from me, had three children, and had experienced a difficult first marriage that had ended. Within three days, we were talking on the phone and within several weeks we saw each other for the first time since our breakup.

After that, our relationship moved like a freight train. Within a few months we committed to spend the rest of our lives together. Three months later she moved to my town. A year later we were married. A year after that we had our beautiful son Dylan.

What I had thought was just the passion of youth was actually eternal passion.

With the passage of time, Erika and I have cultivated the ability to work through the fears and issues that plagued us as kids. We have never had a true problem with each other — anytime we argue it is always about something that is connected to emotional baggage from childhood. Thankfully, we now have the maturity to see that. We also understand enough of what life is like apart so that we will never walk away again. I am with my true love forever.

After Erika and I got back together, my musical passion became truly unleashed. I now write an average of six songs a day, mostly about her, and I am immersed in my creativity. She gave me a new belief in myself and the encouragement to pursue my music as a career, regardless of the consequences.

Who would have predicted where it would lead?

I am now a singer and songwriter who writes and performs with the biggest artists in the world. I am on an upcoming major TV show where I will be working with some of the most talented people in hip-hop. I have my own album that is soon to be released out of Nashville. I've had the privilege and honor to work on it with some of my childhood heroes. My life has been transformed.

So, how does all of this apply to you?

It's simpler than you think.

Face Your Eternal Fear

When you are unhappy, unhealthy, or unfulfilled, often your emotions will be blocked in some way. You may be protecting yourself by avoiding some unpleasant emotions.

What is blocking your emotions?

For me, it was food. Once I removed the blockage, emotions were released that I needed to deal with. When you identify what compulsion is blocking you from your true feelings and remove it, you have two choices:

You can replace that compulsion with another compulsion as I did when I replaced smoking with food.

You can allow the emotions to be released and face the fears you have been avoiding.

How do you do this?

It all starts with looking at your current state of health and well-being. Look at your diet and change the way you eat. Get your body moving and establish a regular program of exercise. After that, the next step is to begin exploring your feelings.

When you feel yourself slipping into old habits, investigate how you are feeling. Let the emotions out so you can start to see what they are. For example, if food is one of your compulsions or crutches, eventually you will find yourself desperate to cheat on this new way of eating—it will happen—but before you do, ask yourself a simple question:

What am I feeling right now?

Am I sad?

Scared?

Angry?

Make sure you answer with what you are *feeling* and not what you are *thinking*.

Next, ask yourself: *Why do I feel this way?*

You have to be completely honest with yourself, no matter how scary or shocking the answer is.

You may have blocked emotions for so long that what you are feeling might surprise you. It might feel like it is coming out of left field. It might not make sense to you right away. That's all right.

Once you accept the truth and confront the anxiety and fear you have been afraid to face, you will finally break through to what your primary purpose in life is supposed to be. This is the struggle that is preventing you from living a completely healthy and happy life. You can overcome it and learn to live happily. If I can do it, anyone can do it.

So once you identify what is ailing you emotionally, how do you overcome it?

Live Unafraid

When I left my first wife, I had nothing against her as a human being; she's a great mom and a good person, but she just wasn't the right fit for me as a life partner. I was judged harshly by friends and family for choosing to leave her.

When Erika and I reconnected, there were some people in my social circle who looked at her with scorn even though she didn't do anything wrong. We just happened to get back together.

I felt their judgment intensely, and that caused me to think:

Am I a bad person?

Am I completely wrong and selfish for this?

In addition, my choice to focus on music received much criticism. I've owned several different businesses, but when I began to choose to follow my music instead, some of my friends and extended family members thought I was losing my mind.

How could I be so foolish to think I could pursue music as a career?

Should it remain a hobby, as I kept hearing from the people in my life?

These people felt that I should focus more on other, more reasonable businesses instead of following my passion. They ridiculed me and judged me. Sadly, I lost relationships with some people who were very close to me because they believed I had gone crazy pursuing this dream.

All of this caused me to have a lot of internal conflict. The people who were criticizing me were people whose opinions I had respected; they were people whose opinions I had valued my whole life. I had looked to them to figure out who I was supposed to be; to let me know if I was doing right or wrong. And they were telling me I was wrong.

Was I really wrong?

It wasn't like I was a drug addict or I was violent or anything like that. I'm a pretty G-rated guy, overall, and I knew I was a good dad.

So, what was going on?

Were these people, whom I trusted, wrong?

Were they being unkind and unfair?

The answer is hard for me to say but it's the truth—it shouldn't be hard to say:

I have a right to be happy. No one else has the right to judge what I am doing to make myself happy as long as I'm not intentionally hurting someone in the process or doing anything illegal.

Last time I checked, creating music and being in love are still legal.

So how does this relate to your life?

After being brave enough to face your emotional fears, whatever they may be, you will have to be brave enough to face the dysfunction around you that caused them to perpetuate.

You will not have to seek out this dysfunction. Once you start living through that emotional blockage you will be absolutely shocked at what reveals itself; you will clearly see which people aren't comfortable with the new you. You will see who wants you to succeed.

It may be a very difficult time for you, as it was for me.

The key is to be strong enough in your heart. Know in your heart that you are not wrong for trying to live a different way. Know you are not a bad person for trying to better yourself.

CHAPTER TWO

Family

BEING IN LOVE WITH YOUR LIFE PARTNER

The day I sold my business, everything should have been fine. But it was the worst day of my life. Financially I was in great shape. To the outside world, my wife and I were the picture-perfect couple. Our personalities seemed to gel well. We got along, but I was absolutely miserable.

It took me quite a while to figure out why I was so miserable, but essentially, I was empty inside. She is a good person; we were very friendly with one another, but we never should have been married. We were friends, but there was no passion there.

Some people would have been happy with that, and I understand that. But for me, just existing with somebody that you get along with is not what I want my life to be.

So I made a change. I decided to take a hard look at my life, and I left. I got a lot of criticism for it from many people in my life.

I heard comments like:

"What about the kids?"

"There is really nothing bad going on there; why are you leaving?"

It was because I wasn't happy; I felt empty inside. I didn't want to waste the rest of my life in a relationship that didn't involve love. That's how I felt, honestly. Ending my marriage was the right choice for me.

How do you see *your* relationship?

To explore this part of you, some guidelines and questions to ask yourself are coming up. If you are unhappy, it is important to take a careful look at your relationships, even if it is difficult. Don't avoid thinking about it. Don't be afraid to be brutally honest.

Look inside and ask yourself: *Would the child I was be proud of the person I am?*

When you were growing up, you visualized the relationship you wanted.

1. How close are you to that vision?

2. If you don't have what you want, what is preventing you from having it?

3. What are the roadblocks as to why you are not who you wanted to be?

4. Is there a complacency in your current relationship?

5. Are you in a relationship that on the surface is okay, but it doesn't give you any feelings of passion and joy?

6. Are you with somebody just because it is easier than being alone?

7. Is your relationship causing you to do destructive things that you wouldn't normally do? This includes self-destructive behaviors like overeating, drinking, and wasting time instead of indulging in productive, fulfilling pursuits.

8. Is it the true path you are supposed to be on, or is it a life of escape?

Look at yourself, and be honest with where your relationship is right now.

Codependency

Sometimes relationships persist in large part because the partners are *codependent*. Codependency exists when partners have an unhealthy attachment to each other; the relationship is controlled by the weakest parts of each person rather than by the strongest parts.

A codependency may involve alcoholism or a mental instability, but sometimes they are not so easy to spot. They can exist in very subtle forms.

Are you holding each other back?

Do you see controlling or manipulative behavior?

Are you keeping each other from pursuing endeavors outside your comfort zone?

These conditions may be evidence of a codependency. You have to look hard at your relationship to discover the answers.

Find Love Again

It is possible to find love again — either with your current partner or someone else. Only you know your current situation and how you truly feel about your current partner. Only you know if it is worth trying to bring it back to life. It is critical for you to be painfully honest about this. There are some relationships that don't work; there are couples who are not healthy together.

If you decide that it is possible to bring your relationship back to life, you will have to go back to the beginning and from there, figure out what got you off course along the way.

Here are some questions to ask that may help you assess your relationship:

1. Do you feel hostile, resentful, or just plain bored with your current partner?

2. When you were first dating, was there earth-shattering passion?

3. Do you still have feelings of passion?

4. Were you enamored with this person?

5. Do you share the same interests?

6. Do you have the same views on life?

7. How did your relationship get off track:

    Was it a slow process of life getting in the way?

    Did you neglect each other in favor of other responsibilities?

    Has something egregious occurred that is keeping you apart?

    Have you just grown apart and want different things?

8. Do you encourage each other to go after your dreams?

9. Are you bad for each other's growth:

   Do you allow each other to be out of shape or support other unhealthy behaviors?

   Do you compensate for each other's anxieties?

   Do you have compulsions you appease for one another?

10. Are you with your partner for love, or because your partner fills a need for you?

There is a huge difference between loving someone freely and staying with them because they fill a need for you. The key to being truly in love is to be with someone *by choice*, not necessity.

This can all be very complicated. My first wife and I came to the conclusion, after over a year of trying to resolve our issues, that we were codependent and weren't good for one another. While this is language often used relative to issues of addiction, there was no alcoholism or addiction or anything like that in our relationship.

Codependency usually involves the enabling of destructive or dysfunctional conduct. One of our issues was that I had a lot of obsessive-compulsive behaviors and she functioned as an enabler for me. It was very destructive to our relationship. Ultimately, we couldn't get beyond that issue.

After we broke up, a funny thing happened. My obsessive-compulsive behavior started to go away. Without her as a crutch, that coping mechanism disappeared, and I started to feel again. That's when Erika reappeared as the love of my life.

As I said earlier, Erika and I had a lot of issues from childhood. They interfere with our relationship routinely.

However, the difference between us now as compared with when we were young is that we put in the time and effort, as exhausting as it can be at times, to try to understand each other's perspective without judgment. This is not easy, because it's hard not to take it personally when someone is figuring out their feelings in real time.

Erika and I have our ups and downs, but our newer, more mature relationship is now ten years old. We have more passion and fire for each other today than ever before. We don't ever lose that spark because we make each other the number one priority in each other's life.

We dote on each other, we pay attention to each other, we are each other's biggest fans, and we are fully engaged in each other's lives while allowing each other to have separate lives. It's not easy to do this, but, for us, we have found a way to keep the passion alive and remain wildly in love.

I have come to see that we are able to stay this way mainly because our philosophy is to give our relationship priority above everything else.

Your Life Partner Should Come Above Everything— Including Your Children

I will probably hear a lot of objections to this because common practice dictates that your children should always come first.

Here is the problem with this way of thinking:

When you put your children above your relationship with your partner, you put your life partnership at risk. In making this point, I am not saying that your kids are secondary. But I am saying that in order for you to have a complete, happy family, you have to make your relationship with your life partner your first priority.

If you're not happy, the family won't be happy. The kids aren't going to be happy. There will be dysfunction.

What does it mean to make your relationship your first priority?

A part of this strategy is making time to be together. My wife and I have two date nights a week. We go out every Wednesday night and every Saturday night. We make it a point to do a long weekend somewhere away from the kids once a quarter, and we have a weeklong vacation together at least once a year.

We make sure we spend time together away from the kids to make sure we are in touch with one another. Additionally, we have other things that we do *with* the kids. Making our relationship a priority doesn't mean a lack of focus on our children; our lives are actually quite focused on them. You'll read more about parenting in the next section.

It is important to remember, however, that kids are physically present in your home for eighteen years. Your relationship with your partner could last fifty, sixty, or seventy years.

After the kids have grown and are gone, if you have not devoted time to your partner and made them your priority, what is your relationship going to be like when it is just the two of you in the house?

Being in love with your life partner goes beyond just loving your partner. Be passionate about your life partner. Always make it a point to bring them flowers, write them a card, make them some fine food, or do something loving for that person every day.

I'm not talking about losing yourself and your own identity in the process, but you should be each other's number-one fan; this is a person you should almost put on pedestal. That's the way that you should always come at your relationship. If you do this, you will reap the rewards for the rest of your life.

BEING PRESENT AND ENGAGED WITH YOUR CHILDREN

In this era, parenting has commonly become an intense activity-driven process. When I look back to my own childhood, I see that parents in that generation were largely out finding themselves, and we as children were kind of an afterthought. Many of us ended up fending for ourselves. It wasn't ideal, but the current generation has a different problem that is no less serious.

Our generation seems to have gone in the exact opposite direction. We often think of good parenting as giving everything and anything you possibly can to your kids. From the time of their birth, we are focused on their well-being. We select a variety of intense activities to foster their growth, being sure their brains are stimulated properly and they have proper mental and physical training so they can be at their best — at five years old!

We need to take a step back and look at how overdriven we are.

What is driving this hyperactive parenting?

Are we listening to our kids at all in the process?

Are we getting to know our kids?

Pursue What Your Children Love

When I was a child, I played one sport in the fall and one sport in the spring. That was the extent of my organized activity as a child. Nowadays it seems like kids play twelve different sports including traveling leagues — which didn't even exist when I was a kid — so now people spend their whole weekends in far-away towns watching their kid play games.

To me, this is not a healthy situation for children or parents. We need to look carefully at our shared activities and reassess their value.

Does a seven-year-old child truly know what they are passionate about and what they want their lives to be?

Do they want their weekends to be spent playing soccer off in other towns or at baseball or ballet camps?

Or do they really desire interaction with their parents?

I coached my kids in every sport they've ever played. As the years went on, I noticed that my sons were wanting to play football and baseball, etc., more to hang out with me than actually to play the sports.

I realized this fully one season when I said I wasn't going to coach that year. They ended up not wanting to play the sport anymore simply because I wasn't going to be the coach.

It was a revelation: My children enjoyed playing, but to them, the most valuable part of the sport was *the bonding experience with me*.

Since then, I have reversed course on this part of my parenting. I don't schedule activities to fill their time.

Now I ask them what they *want* to do and really try to listen to the answers:

What do you guys like?

You're getting older now; what do you want to pursue?

Now I am engaged with what they love as opposed to me trying to fit in the activities that I think they are going to like because I love them.

It's a very subtle but a vitally important shift in thinking. If I'm going to interact with my kids, it's going to be based on what *their* interests are. For example, one of my sons is currently into mathematics and mythology — Greek, Roman, Chinese, Hindu, Norse, and so on. Another of my sons loves photography and directing.

Now I spend a lot of time finding different activities that engage my children in the areas where their passions lie, and this is joyful and fulfilling for all of us.

We have a tendency to want to drill into our kids' heads what we think they need to know. But they all have the ability to see for themselves what they actually like and want to learn about. We need to make sure we are interacting with them based on what matters to them as opposed to what we want them to be.

Give Children the Tools to Do for Themselves Instead of Always Doing for Them

My wife and I have six children together. At this point, we have three eleven-year-olds, two eight-year-olds, and a five-year-old. She had three in her first marriage, I had two in mine, and we have one together. Big families are not common in our generation. We are looked at like we have nine heads for having six kids. It wasn't by design. But it is what it is, and we love every insane minute of it.

What it has forced us to do is to offer our kids more independence than most kids of their generation. In addition to the extreme amount of activities, parents in our generation tend to do everything for their children. It is well-intentioned, of course, but the result is a delay in children learning to take care of themselves.

We have focused on helping our kids become self-sufficient. They wake up in the morning, they know how to make their own breakfast, and they look out for one another. In addition to being capable and independent, they have become adaptable and imaginative. My wife is wonderful with them; she dotes on them, cooks and cares for them, but also allows them to learn to fend for themselves as they grow.

My wife and I do not set up a lot of organized play or activities for them. These six kids spend all day just being kids. They'll go outside and play these imaginative, inventive games. One time, our son Brice tried to build a time machine out of a red wagon and other supplies. It was wonderful. He and his siblings spent an entire day trying to build a working time machine.

Last summer, they spent half the summer filming an entire movie. Each one of them has their own iPad, and they had the idea of using each one as a camera, so they created a film with six different camera angles. They used a fog machine and independently built the props, including a coffin. They had a wonderful time, all one hundred percent organized by them. It was super cool.

Sadly, these kinds of experiences are very much outside the norm for kids these days. We don't allow kids to orchestrate their own activities very often. Many parents are overprotective. What they think will benefit their child actually gets in the way of parenting — likely a byproduct of all the information we get from TV and the Internet.

It is important to note that allowing children independence doesn't mean leaving them unsupervised. You can still be home and be present but allow your kids to have a sense of autonomy so they can grow into adults with the tools to achieve success.

Do we want our children to need their parents forever, as a constant crutch?

Of course we don't. We don't want this whole generation to be self-entitled and helpless. We want them to be adults who are self-sufficient, happy, and fulfilled.

LIVING AS AN EXAMPLE TO YOUR CHILDREN

When I analyze how to raise my children, I look back at my own childhood and think about what knowledge I gleaned as a child.

How did I learn best from my parents?

Was it what my mom and my dad told me, or was it from watching their examples?

If you actually truly clear your mind and think about the learning that impacted you the most, it's almost always things you saw, felt, or experienced—not the things you were told. True knowledge does not really come from someone telling you; it's always more about you seeing examples of it, internalizing it, and living it for yourself.

If you truly want to impart the best examples to your kids, it's going to be through the way you live your life.

Stop Preaching and Start Teaching

Instead of lecturing your kids on how they should do *this* and not do *that*, the best way to teach your children is to show them the way. If you want your child to pursue certain things or understand right from wrong, you have to demonstrate these actions yourself.

Before you can do this, you may have to look at your own life and start making some assessments about yourself and your own behavior.

If somebody is drinking a six-pack of beer every night but telling their kids not to drink because it is bad for them, will the message really get across?

If you are out smoking a cigarette on the back porch and are telling them not to smoke or do drugs, think about the mixed message you are giving them.

The way to stop preaching and start teaching is to look inward. If you are not living the way you're telling your kids to live, then you need to start by correcting your own behaviors first.

I know that is easier said than done, but if your ultimate goal is to be a good parent to your own kids, how can you be that without showing them a good path forward?

None of us is perfect. Of course we all have bad habits.

But are we attempting to correct these behaviors?

Can our children see this?

We all have failures, limitations, or flaws, but the goal of this life is to achieve better, to try to become the best self that we can, whatever that means to each person. That is the best way to trying to go about teaching them, instead of just preaching to them what they should be.

How You Live Life Is How Your Children Will Live Life

Beyond good or bad, how you live your life is how your children will live their lives to a certain extent. They are going to set their priorities similarly to what your priorities are.

For example, my mom left when I was eight or nine, and I was raised by my dad for a good chunk of my childhood. I watched how he lived his life. He never did anything that really made him happy. He just did what he thought he had to do to support a family and what in his mind was perceived as doing the right thing.

I watched my father countless times in his life talk about the things he always wanted to do but never pursued. He stayed in a nine-to-five job, doing what he thought he had to do to get a paycheck. He had a quiet misery to him.

When I grew up, I did the same thing. I didn't pursue the things that I loved. I pursued business and careers, and I was very good at them fortunately, but this way of living life made me miserable. I went this way because I thought it was something that was expected of me.

At a certain age, something snapped inside of me, and I thought: *This is ridiculous. Is this really the right way to live?*

I was throwing my life away in pursuit of something that I didn't even care about. I made a change in who I was; I started pursuing a career that made more sense to me — my music — and started on the road to being an artist, a singer, and a songwriter.

I think this has had a fundamental impact on my children.

My unspoken message to them wasn't, "You need to be artistic."

The message was, "You need to pursue what you love."

Watching me pursue my passions helps give my kids the freedom to pursue their passions. Instead of doing what I thought I was supposed to do, I did what I felt passionate about. I see my kids having the same freedom inside of them to pursue what they love. Whether your passion is photography or mathematics, life is about pursuing what is inside of you instead of just doing what you think you are supposed to do.

Let Your Kids See You Be Human

In our society, there is a certain level of protection expected of parents, but the common sentiment is that we need to shelter our kids from all bad things. Often we also shelter them from our own struggles and failures.

To some extent, it is reasonable to keep your kids out of harm's way, but to sanitize life and make kids feel like there is no such thing as failure is a disservice to kids. It doesn't give them the tools they need to live a well-rounded life and overcome adversity. Understanding that people have weak moments will help your children deal with their own.

Often parents are afraid to allow their children to learn to lose. Games in which everyone is a winner and everyone gets a certificate have become common. To me, this results in children never learning about overcoming adversity.

If all you do is win constantly, you are never given a moment where you have to struggle to overcome difficulty. And this is one of the keys to life. It's not about winning or losing; it is about overcoming adversity.

Let your kids have moments where they battle back. Moreover, allow your kids to be engaged in your life, your ups, your downs, and your struggles — appropriately, of course, based on their ages — so that they can understand from your life that you have struggles, too. They will see that struggle is natural in life, and obstacles can be overcome.

In recent years, my kids have watched me record my own album in the room above my garage and witnessed my ensuing struggles to succeed in the music industry. They watched the ups and downs and frustrations for four years. I let them see my pursuit.

They felt it.

They have had their moments of thinking: *Daddy is going to make it now,* and they've also been there to witness some disappointments.

It's okay for your kids to see you fail. But they must also see you continuing to try.

You get back up and do it again, and this shows them that it's okay to fail. It shows them that if you believe in what you are doing and get knocked in the face, you should just keep going.

If you don't give your kids those tools, they won't ever be able to handle stress. So much that comes at you in life is not easy. Struggle is natural. If your children don't learn this from you, they will always accept the easy route as the only one possible. When they become adults, so much happiness and fulfillment will be out of reach for them if they always take the easy route.

In general, living as an example to your children means making sure that they see you have a life of purpose. They will see you pursuing what you think is your best path. Allowing them to see the good, the bad, the ugly, warts and all, is the best way to teach your kids how they can live their futures.

Being engaged and present to your children will enhance your life and theirs.

Keep these ideas in mind:

- Talk to your children about what they are interested in.

- Focus more on *interaction* than *activity*.

- Teach your children self-sufficiency.

- Give your children freedom to explore their world independently.

- Allow your children to fail so they can learn to get back up again.

- Use your life as an example for your children.

- Let them see you struggle sometimes, but keep trying.

- Encourage them to do what they love.

CHAPTER **THREE**

Work

FIND SOMETHING THAT YOU LOVE TO DO AND THAT INSPIRES YOU

Throughout my life, I have had a lot of successes. I've owned software companies and medical practices. I've been a successful businessman.

As time has passed, I have realized that successes resulting from chasing the almighty dollar cannot not buy you happiness. Going after something you love instead of going after money is how you achieve ultimate fulfillment in life.

So how do you figure out how to do what you love?

Start out by answering this question:

If You Had a Billion Dollars, What Would You Do with Your Life?

When I ask this question of people, I'm always amazed how much of a revelation it is for them. It is a useful way of figuring out what truly makes you happy.

If you had all the money in the world, what would you do with your time?

When someone has an immediate response to the question, usually it is very specific. Perhaps they would work for a particular charitable cause, pursue something in the arts, or start a small business where they are making something specific — say, bicycles, for example.

Many people actually will be able to visualize immediately what they would want to do if they didn't have to worry about money anymore.

If you take a step back and ask yourself that question and you can answer it, *you just figured out what you should be doing with your life.*

However, the next thing people usually say is, "That is unrealistic. I can't make money doing that."

They are so sure of this, even though they haven't tried.

Well, I'm here to tell you that that is not true. In 2009, I had owned multiple businesses, and I was a frustrated musician. I hadn't done anything significant with my music in years. I decided to pursue it. Everybody thought I was crazy, but after working with some of the biggest artists on the planet — writing, recording, producing, owning and starring in a TV show that is on a major cable network; and having my own dreams come true. I am here to tell you that it is all possible.

How to Pursue Your Dream

There are three important elements to pursuing your dream. They are listed below and I will discuss each of them further:

- Immerse yourself in your craft.
- Ask for what you want.
- Show up; always be present.

First, you must completely immerse yourself in your craft. Whatever it is that you are going to do, you have to be completely engaged in it. Remember, *it takes ten thousand hours of doing something to become a master of it.*

Secondly, you always have to ask for what you want. When you're pursuing your dream, you can't be timid. You have to ask for what you want in life, because if you leave things up to other people to decide for you, then your life is going to be decided for you without any input from you.

Be plainspoken, blunt, and direct, and when you are pursuing what you want, be specific. You have to ask for exactly what you are looking for.

More important than anything else, you have to show up. You have to be there. You have to be present. Remember that 80 percent of success is just showing up! I can't tell you how many times I've had amazing opportunities present themselves to me just by showing up.

All of these elements sound like clichés, but this is because they are universal truths.

Two weeks ago, I was in Nashville. I went to a charity event, and I was going to meet one of the most prolific songwriters of all time, Desmond Child. He wrote *You Give Love a Bad Name, Livin' on a Prayer, Livin' La Vida Loca* and many other songs. I almost didn't go because I was nervous to meet him. But I did finally decide to go, and met him, and amazingly, we discovered we have some things in common that led to another opportunity.

I'm a Cuban guy who grew up in New Jersey, and Desmond is a Cuban guy who wrote most of his songs in New Jersey. In addition, he is currently in the middle of making a play called *Cuba Libre* for Broadway. One of the roles he will be casting in his play is Fidel Castro and we talked about the fact that I'm actually related to Fidel. After meeting me, he was intrigued by how much I look like the man. After our meeting, he asked me to audition for the part of Fidel in his play.

I don't know where it's going to lead; it may lead to nothing. But the point is, it's another opportunity that I never would have gotten if I didn't show up.

Looking Backward to Go Forward

You may know that you are not doing what you love, but may be having a hard time figuring out how to find where you are meant to be. Looking back at your young life may help you.

Think about this poignant question:

Would the boy or girl you were be proud of the man or woman you are?

Go back to when you were young, but old enough to be thinking about who you wanted to be when you grew up. Go backward and get yourself back into that moment of life, to the kind of understanding you possessed when you had nothing else clouding your judgment. As a child, you were innocent and completely present in everyday life; you were living in the moment. That part of you probably knows better than you know yourself now.

Go back to those feelings and figure out what mattered most to you then, outside of the obvious children's things, of course.

When you looked forward then, what did you envision for your life?

Now look at that and ask yourself:

Okay, is that something I can still pursue now?

Now, if you are fifty years old and you wanted to be a basketball player in the NBA, well, that dream might not be practical. But you can still find the other interests and what you have lost along the way. You will be absolutely amazed at how looking back can help you.

This is one of the ways I got back in tune with my mind. It all happened because I bought a car that was a stick shift instead of an automatic, as silly as this sounds. As a kid, all we ever had were stick shifts, but ever since then, I have driven nothing but automatics. So when I got an old car that was a stick shift, it opened something in my brain.

I started driving and all of a sudden, I was thrown back into that seventeen—or eighteen-year-old kid again. Somehow it opened parts of my brain that had been lying dormant and helped me get back in tune with my teenage passionate self. Something that simple had such a profound effect.

Looking backward does not mean just look at what you wanted, but immerse yourself in things you used to do as a child and a teenager. Bring that mindset back, and then go from there.

People most often block themselves from going after what inspires them because of a fear of feeling foolish.

Is it foolish to go after what you love?

Of course not. Remember, however, that if you are going to go after a life of passion and happiness, you must be ready to have a lot of people tell you what a fool you are. You have to get past those feelings if you want to be happy because nobody else knows what is going to make you happy but you.

Sometimes other people just won't understand. Sometimes people will look at you with a very judgmental eye because you are doing something that they would like to do, but are too afraid pursue for themselves. Set all the criticism aside, focus on where your happiness will come from, and don't doubt yourself.

PICK SOMETHING NOT BASED ON YOUR EXPERIENCE, A PAYCHECK, OR A DOLLAR AMOUNT

As I said in the previous chapter, you may want to set aside a lot of the education and knowledge that you gleaned in the career you have been pursuing. If it is not not satisfying you, then it probably is not the wheelhouse you want to be in.

Everything that you have learned in life can be useful to you in some way, but you need to decide which of those things you want to build upon. Sometimes it's okay to do a complete short circuit and go somewhere new.

How do you step outside of your current self without sacrificing it?

How do you learn to figure out what to do without being boxed in by what you've already done?

Follow Your Passion Instead of Your Fear

I have a terrible habit that has plagued me for most of my adult life: I have a great knack for seeing an opportunity in business and going full bore into pursuing it.

Why is this a terrible habit?

Because I always seem to get distracted from what I love to do and want to pursue; I see an opportunity to make money.

The problem I have is rooted in fear. I am always very fearful that my pursuit of happiness in my career is going to cause financial harm and disruption to my wife and kids.

It is easy for me to make unemotional, objective business decisions about the things for which I have no passion or interest. When it comes to my life and my career, the hardest belief for me to have faith in is that by doing what I love to do, I can provide for my family just as well as if I were chasing the other money-making prospects I don't really care about.

The irony is that as I look back at my career, I realize I might be good at seeing opportunities, but, more often than not, if it is something I don't have a passion for, I will not be successful.

For me to be successful, I have to be truly passionate about what I am doing. My experiences have ingrained in me that I am that guy who pursues good opportunities — but the truth is that I am much better at being an artist and pursuing my passions instead of chasing money. Just because you have done something for a number of years doesn't mean it's what you're good at or what you *should be* doing. Set that aside, and go find what it is that you truly love to do.

How to Figure Out Your Financial Goals

Many people make their choice of career based on fear. They aren't thinking about what they want to do, but are only thinking about getting their basic needs supported.

If you have that mindset, you're playing *not to lose* instead of playing *to win*.

If you've already been working for a while, it can be even more difficult to get away from your current path. It may feel much easier to simply stay where you are.

These kinds of thoughts might go through your head when you think about changing your situation:

I have all of these years of experience so I can make x dollars a year and be comfortable.

It's enough for me.

I can put money aside for fun things if I just keep doing this same thing.

It doesn't really matter if it's something I don't like to do.

I have to do things I don't like to make money.

I don't necessarily hate this job; it's not that bad.

I'll just do this long enough to be able to retire and then I'll enjoy my life.

This mindset is the absolute wrong way of thinking. It is the absolute wrong way to live. I don't care what they say about how wealth is created by saving a little bit, year after year. That all sounds well and good, but it isn't. You need to see that happiness and fulfillment are *also* forms of wealth. Happiness and fulfillment are creative and vital pursuits.

If you are playing a waiting game, think about all the years going by, waiting for you to have enough money to chill out.

After that, what are you going to do with your life?

You will have squandered most of your life pursuing a dream that will only manifest itself when you are old.

Set all of those preconceived notions aside, and don't think about what you need for the moment. Don't think about what you fear for the moment. Think about what you *want*.

What will you find fulfilling?

Money?

Pursuing your passion?

Relaxing?

Think about what you love to do and what you can imagine being a fulfilling career. Then think about your financial goals.

Do you want a billion dollars?

What will it take to get there?

Work backwards in your mind. Instead of thinking about what you can buy if you keep earning money, think about your goals.

How can you use what you love to do to achieve those goals?

Do you want a gargantuan mansion?

Take a step back. Stop worrying about what you need financially just to get by. Throw that out the window, and focus on going after with gusto whatever it is that you want.

How to Harness Your Unused Talents to Get to Where You Want to Be

As I mentioned earlier, I've been a songwriter for years, and I play twelve instruments. But there was a ten- to fifteen-year period in my life where I wrote few songs. It was because it wasn't what I was focused on. I wasn't tapped into my own emotions. I was chasing money.

When I reconnected with my fiancé from college and we got back together, everything changed.

Erika is my forever-muse. Being with her unleashed something inside of me, and the songs started pouring out again. When I first started writing, it was a song every couple of days or weeks, whatever it was; and I cobbled together a fourteen-song album in a year. I wrote maybe forty or fifty songs over the course of that year, which seems pretty good.

But as I have been doing this more and more and more, I have found that I have the ability to write six to ten songs a day. God has given me this gift. I can write a hook to a song, like a very catchy chorus, with a melody and the basic structure of a song, in about two minutes.

This is such a gift because I can put together a structure of a song and then work with an artist, leaving the verses open for them to express themselves. But it has worked for me, and I have achieved a lot of success in that regard.

Everything that I've been discussing in this chapter goes to this root question:

How do you harness your unused talents to get where you want to be?

In my case, the unharnessed talent was this ridiculous wealth of catchy little rhymes inside of me. Up until five years ago, I didn't recognize that I was skilled at writing lyrics.

You have a unique talent.

What is it?

What is that unique thing that you can do, even if it seems like a parlor trick that you do at parties?

Think about that one unique thing that we all have that you pull out when you want to make yourself stand out from a crowd.

Got it?

Start developing it.

PURSUE SOMETHING OUTSIDE YOUR COMFORT ZONE

We all get into a rhythm or routine. Some would call it a rut. We wake up in the morning, go about our days following a routine, come home and go to bed. We get into habits, become comfortable, and gain a sense of familiarity with our day-to-day lives.

The habitual existence gives us the illusion of control, and it's hard to break out of such a comfortable routine. It is necessary for you to do this, however, in order to make changes in your life.

Have Faith That You Can Be Good at What You Love

For years, I didn't do much with my music. I knew I had talent, but I had assumed I squandered it. When I started getting back into it, and I put together my first album, I put it out on the Internet and made a video. I pursued it. I took a leap of faith that other people would care about anything I had to say musically.

It was a difficult leap.

After all, who was I?

I was somebody who was relatively old to get into the music game. I hadn't done anything of significance or substance in music since I was eighteen. Back in the day, my band had opened up for a pretty big musical act. But that was years ago. Nobody knew who I was.

When I put my music out into the world, I took a leap of faith that people would care about what I did and think it was good. It has led me on the most wonderful path. After releasing the album, I made a hard left from rock into hip-hop, did some writing with some of the biggest hip-hop artists of all time, ended up on a major TV show, then veered back into southern rock and country to be able to do an album in my own right.

I went down a winding road all the way back to where I wanted to be in the first place. It took that wacky road to get to where I am now.

You have to keep faith in yourself, even if the road you are on takes some unpredictable turns. The point is that you shouldn't give up; don't give up on your path just because it was not what you initially had in mind.

Look at Your Social Circle

Schoolyard politics play out in adult life as well. After you get comfortable with a group of friends, this group of friends also gets comfortable with a preconceived notion of who you are and who you are supposed to be. You might be boxed in by their ideas of you and your reputation.

You may get dragged down by the people around you — they may think they know what is best for you and what you should be doing.

They aren't trying to hurt you or hold you back. They all think they are being good friends to you. Everybody does this. When you have known people for twenty years, you think you know what makes them tick and what makes them happy.

The truth is, most of us hide some of who we really are and what we really want, especially from our friends. We buy into notions of things that we don't necessarily believe or feel just because we want to gain approval and have people like us.

If you feel that you are in a situation where you're surrounded by people more so because you get approval from them, rather than because they truly do understand who you are, you need to take a step back and perhaps pursue some different social contacts.

Look at the people surrounding you.

If you have a certain hobby or passion that you want to pursue, are these the people who will help you pursue it?

For me, I had the greatest friends on the planet from my college days, my old fraternity brothers. They are good guys, white-collar guys who worked nine-to-five jobs. I've never had a nine-to-five job in my life.

People think this is because I'm a natural entrepreneur, and maybe there's some truth to that, but when I went that way right out of college, it was out of survival because I could never work for anybody. I'm too stubborn and can't stand authority.

But I got branded by my friends as *the guy who owned businesses.*

That was me. When I got back into music and started pursuing my passions, these guys thought I had absolutely lost my mind. They couldn't understand it. It wasn't them, it was totally me; I had revealed who I really was, and they didn't recognize me anymore.

I didn't walk away from my friends, and they didn't walk away from me. We just drifted for a while, but, now we are back in each other's lives with a different perspective; and they accept me for me, and I am truly grateful for that.

In addition, I now have made friends with people who pursue similar interests, but they come in and out of my life also. Now I'm with people in my life in the moment because there is something we should be doing together and not just because of our history together.

Seek Engagement with New People and Situations

Jonathan Hay, a publicist who used to work for Rihanna, produced my album, which was very rock-oriented. We started working together, producing together, and we worked very well together. We became friends. I owned a record label with him.

He wanted to sign a group, Horseshoe GANG, that was composed of four kids who were in rap and hip-hop.

They made an album called *Knockin' on Rap's Door*. I thought that was a pretty cool take on the Bob Dylan song *Knockin' on Heaven's Door*, but they had never actually heard the Dylan song. I played it for them, and they loved it.

These kids were the brothers of a guy who was in a group called Slaughterhouse, a pretty well-known group, although the guy was not someone I was familiar with. As a result of my interactions with his brothers, I was introduced to him, Kxng Crooked.

To put it simply, that introduction was the impetus for me veering into hip-hop.

In addition, meeting Kxng Crooked was the catalyst for my creating a TV show.

He told me about his idea for the show, which was like a hip-hop *American Idol*. My wife and I sat with him and decided it was an amazing idea. We got the financing together and ran with it. He pulled in Sway Calloway and King Tech, major talents in hip-hop. I persuaded other great artists I had worked with to join the project.

I certainly had no idea that signing these four complete unknown kids would lead me to their brother, who would lead me to this huge opportunity with a major

TV show. If I hadn't been open to new people and different situations, it never would have happened.

Do something different. Meet new people. If you have never played tennis before, play tennis. Whatever it is, start doing things that are completely out of the ordinary for you. Don't say no to anything. Experience new things. You will be thrilled to see where they can lead.

CHAPTER FOUR

Passion

PASSION WITH YOUR LIFE PARTNER

Have you caught the theme of my life yet?

I live like the Greeks of old. When somebody died in old Greek society, the highest compliment one could make about the person was that they had lived a life of passion. Ultimately, if you're not pursuing or being in love, you're not really living life. You should go at everything in life with passion.

What's more important than being passionate about your life partner?

Who is more important than the person you want to spend the rest of your life with?

If you're not going to pursue that relationship in earnest, what else will you pursue in earnest?

Be Madly In Love

As time goes by, it is so easy to become:

- Complacent
- Blasé
- Comfortable
- Unconcerned about your looks
- Out of shape
- Forgetful of what makes you feel sexy

It's easy to lose that fire with your partner that you had when you were first dating.

We all know that moment when you first set eyes on the person you fell in love with, that feeling of:

Holy cow, I'm wild about this person; they're all I can think about.

At some point, for everyone, that feeling seems to subside.

There are a billion books that say these changes are to be expected. There is that first engaged moment, and then everything settles, and it's okay; it's a normal pattern.

Absolutely not!

That is the absolute worst advice that you could ever receive in your life.

Look, obviously when you are with someone for many years, there is a familiarity that forms into a deeper bond. However, *that doesn't mean that the passion goes away.*

My wife and I probably kiss each other one-hundred-and-twenty times a day. When I say kiss, I mean a passionate kiss. It's what we do. At any table, we sit next to each other and constantly hold hands and are constantly touching each other. People think that we just started dating three weeks ago, and they can't believe we have been together for many years. It blows their minds because we are always all over each other.

And that is not only because we want to be, but also because we have made it an absolute point in our relationship to never, ever veer from that.

If one person starts pulling away a little, the other pulls them back to say, "Absolutely not. Get back over here."

We make that a point. We have to always feel that feeling of mad love for each other. When we are apart, we need to feel that sadness.

Ronald Reagan used to say that when he was speaking and Nancy Reagan would leave the room, he would feel his heart break when she would leave. He would have this sadness wash over him.

Regardless of your politics, nobody should deny that those two had a great relationship. It is for that exact reason. You look at Nancy watching Ron give a speech, and you could tell they had a love affair. All of their kids would say it. Some of their kids were probably jealous of their relationship because of it.

The point I'm getting at is that my wife and I are constantly madly in love with each other. We stay in shape. We make sure that we are fun with each other. We flirt with each other constantly. We never let that go away.

Be Madly In Life Together

Being madly *in life* together means not just being in love with one another, which is great when you feel that passion, but also being fully engaged in each other's lives.

There are three parts of the puzzle there:

1. Your life together, your relationship
2. Your activities
3. Your family

In a couple, both people have their individual lives. That is critical. Each person has to maintain their own independence, their sovereignty, and the things that they love. You should be the biggest advocate and fan of whatever your life partner's other pursuits are, as scary and freaky as some of that can be.

My wife is the most amazing person I have ever met. She has fear sometimes about my being an artist and my traveling and playing gigs. That fear factor about me being away from home and having fans is reasonable. But she doesn't allow that to get in her head and limit me from doing what I love. I am forever grateful to her for that patience and understanding.

My wife is a dancer; she owns a performing arts school. She struggles with dividing attention among teaching, choreography, and being a full-time mom. At times the kids need to be with her at work and that requires her to juggle her responsibilities. Sometimes her pursuit of her passion keeps her from being home as much as she wants to be, but she does her best to balance it.

Erika is not the greatest with numbers. She is stunningly beautiful, artistically talented, an amazing mom, and the kindest person I have ever known; but when it comes to making the dollars and cents make sense, she just doesn't have it. Luckily, I have these skills, so together, we make it work.

On the other hand, I am a good businessman, musician, and singer, but I am a horrible reader into the character of people. I will get robbed blind constantly by people because I am super naïve. I meet someone and always see the good in them, but I never see the con artist.

My wife has the most amazing instincts, so if she looks at me and says, "You can't do business with that person," I don't even question it.

But that requires her to be engaged in my life and be a part of it so she can assess the people I am doing business with and keep me out of danger.

We have cultivated a symbiotic relationship in which we are not controlling one another but are being complementary to one another's pursuits. Therefore, we have to be constantly engaged in each other's lives.

Don't Be Afraid to Argue

A lot of people have the idea that a good relationship is evidenced by not having disagreements, getting along all the time.

That is one hundred percent wrong.

If a couple never disagrees or argues, one of three things is going on:

1. There are some serious issues in the relationship that both parties want to avoid dealing with, so they don't argue about anything.

2. There is a very one-sided relationship and thus a dependency exists in which one person is dominating the relationship, and the other person is appeasing them.

3. There is a lack of caring. Whatever the person wants to do, you don't care; and whatever you want to do, they don't care.

Obviously, these are three examples of a relationship in trouble. If you are in a good relationship, do not fear disagreements. They are natural. If you are two strong people who are close to one another, you will have arguments. By arguments, I don't mean yelling; I mean debate.

There is absolutely nothing wrong with disagreement. Part of the beauty of being in a relationship with someone else is having the benefit of seeing their point of view. If you are uncomfortable hearing a different point of view, this is something you need to address in yourself. It is not a measure of a bad relationship; it is a measure of your own insecurity.

Arguing and debating can be amazing. That is how you learn different things about one another and understand more about each other and the world around you.

Don't scream; don't be insulting. But go ahead and disagree, be okay with disagreeing, hear each other's sides, compromise, and move on. Enjoy your life with each other, knowing that sometimes it will be what you want it to be and sometimes it won't.

PASSION AND YOUR CHILDREN

I have talked a lot about your relationship with your kids already, and a lot of what I have touched on in the previous chapters is applicable to this chapter. Be passionate about your relationship with kids just like you are passionate about your love relationship and passionate about your life.

Be madly in love with your child for who they are, not who you want them to be. Don't look at your children as a moniker of who you are. Don't live vicariously through them for the things you didn't get to accomplish. Be engaged with your kids and passionate about who they are because they are their own individual beings.

Be Actively Engaged in Their Passions

As I touched on before, when you are passionately engaged in your children's passions, go beyond interacting with them and get to know what they love. If you see a course of life opening for your child that they want to pursue, open the floodgates to them. Don't push them, just help open the gates.

We know that sometimes kids have interests that change week to week, but some of them will continue for years, or perhaps, for a lifetime. If your daughter wants to be a model, you don't have to take her to the Ford modeling agency in the next week. She is a child, after all, so start with the appropriate building blocks.

When they express an interest, don't push it down and don't ignore it, but you don't need to go over the top with it. Start from the basics and get them some information.

For example, my son started doing stand-up comedy skits. It was really cute. It was great. He was awesome. I just looked at him and told him I would go online and show him some more famous comedians. I showed him some skits from Billy Crystal, Robin Williams, Steve Martin, and Bill Cosby.

I explained to him a few things you need to realize when you are doing stand-up. I used the skits to show him that there is a start, a middle, and a finish to a joke. He enjoyed watching and learning these things with me, and then his interest dissipated with time. But it was a great experience.

My daughter Eliana wanted to pursue modeling. I told her I thought that was cool. I talked with her about the lifestyle, the traveling, and the physical demands. I tried to get her to see that if she wanted to pursue this career, there would be certain things she would have to do and that she would have to fully understand everything that comes with it before she made her decision.

When your kids bring up something they want to pursue, make sure that they understand from the beginning what they will have to do, so that they understand the practical aspects, and it is just not a romantic notion. Let them know that you will be supportive. Be motivational and encouraging.

Although we've talked about some parenting guidelines that are the same across the board, children have individual personalities and require different parenting techniques.

My middle daughters have varied interests and talents. When my daughter Eva started developing a passion for gymnastics, my wife was very hesitant about this because Eva dances as well, and Erika didn't want anything to interfere with that.

However, one day we saw Eva bending and contorting her body and doing backbends, and we asked where she learned to do that. She informed us that she was watching gymnastic instructional videos on YouTube. There is no stopping Eva when she decides she wants to do something. Erika put her in gymnastics class the following week.

My daughter Abby has her own gifts as well. She is precocious at writing and producing a song. She understands the music production software GarageBand better than I could dream to, and she is only eight years old.

The funny thing is that she is the opposite of Eva; she can be easily distracted and convince herself that she wants to pursue things not because she is good at them but, because some other child is good at it, and she wants that praise as well.

So as good parents, our job is to help Abby learn to discern what she wants for herself and what she wants because of others.

Be Madly In Love with Your Kids

Being madly in love with your kids essentially means the same thing as being madly in love with your life partner:

- Be with them
- Be around them
- Learn to understand the things that they love
- Revel in the time that you have with them
- Learn their idiosyncrasies
- Learn the things they laugh at
- Treasure all the memories

A lot of people in my generation don't have the time or the ability to be that engaged with their kids. They lose sight of sharing the smaller things in life with their kids, replacing these interactions with a plethora of organized activities.

What does a good parent do?

Here are some of what I have learned from my children.

To be a good parent:

- Engage with your kids regularly.

- Get to know your children well.

- Watch TV with your kids, and talk with them about the shows they like.

- Play outdoors with your children.

- Get to know your children's friends and what their interests are.

- Be aware of the social media your kids are involved with.

Your children's social circles may be difficult for you to follow. It's very different being a parent in 2016 than any other time in the history of this world. Many kids don't go outside a lot, and they may not even have a lot of in-person interactions.

Social media changes all the time. Recently, Instagram has been the medium of choice, so currently, kids aren't talking on the phone much or even texting. Instagram is all about posting a picture, collecting likes and conversing about it online. But next month, some other platform could be all the rage.

In order for you to be engaged and know your children, you have to be a part of 2016 society whether you like it or not. Otherwise, you are not going to have any clue about what is going on with your kids.

However you can do it, make sure you're spending time truly getting to know your kids. It is the little things that we take for granted that are most important. Talk and joke and play with them. Those are the moments that you actually get to know your kids.

Accept Them, Accept Them, Accept Them

The best gift you can give your children is *your acceptance of who they are*. I can't say this enough. The hardest thing for children—and most adults—to overcome is judgment and fear of letting people down.

Where does the essence of fear and letting people down come from?

It comes from expectations.

What are expectations?

Expectations come from our judgment of what somebody else *should* be doing.

If you look at your own life and think about what your parents' approval has meant to you, you'll probably agree this is a huge issue. Everyone has always wanted their mother's or father's approval in their lives.

What causes us not to have their approval?

Outside of doing anything illegal or criminal or destructive for yourself or your family, parents often can have a preconceived notion of what they want their kids to be. When a child deviates from that preconceived notion, that can earn them disapproval and judgment.

Fear of disapproval can become a bottleneck for our children. It can keep them from going out and actually pursuing what they love and who they want to be. As a parent, you need to do your best to guard against that.

You have to accept your kids for who they are. At the same time, you can't let them sit around and be lazy. You have to find a balance.

How do we strike the proper balance?

What I am saying is that if your kids' passion is to make hot dogs and that is what they want to do, accept it.

Don't let yourself say something like, "You are getting

an A+ in calculus. Why aren't you becoming an engineer?"

That doesn't matter. They are madly passionate about making hot dogs. Go with it. It's cool. There is nothing wrong with that.

Whatever it is you feel is a pinnacle for success, whether it is money, being successful in the arts, or being a great educator, your child may have different feelings about that. Let that be okay with you.

If their pursuit is not money but the arts, and you're a day trader, accept them.

If their pursuit is money and you're a college professor, accept them.

Let it be. They are their own individual beings, and the best gift you can give your child is acceptance of who they are and who they want to be.

PASSION IN YOUR WORK

Outside of passion with your life partner and passion with your children, the next most critical thing is what you spend eight to twelve hours a day doing with your life, and that is your work. We all have to work. We all have to make money. Choose something you can be passionate about.

If you are doing something for most of your day that you don't love and aren't passionate about, it is going to permeate the rest of your existence.

It is going to beat you down day after day, year after year, and it is going to make you feel like you are just existing and not living.

Go back and re-read the last section about *acceptance* in your relationship with your children and apply it to yourself. It is critical for you to accept yourself for who you are, and for who you want to be.

Hard to Get Out of Bed? Change Your Job

If you are working for the weekend, you should not be doing that job. Depending on what your weekend pursuits are, you may want to reverse this situation.

Whatever it is that you want to do on the weekend, would you do it for a job if you had a billion dollars sitting in the bank?

If so, maybe that is what you should be pursuing.

Granted, some people will say, "What I love to do is float in a lake and drink beer."

Or, "I love to spend ninety-seven hours chasing a little ball around a golf course."

Those aren't exactly pursuits that can make you money, depending on where you are at in life. But take a step back.

Are those pursuits, or are they escapes?

An escape is not what you truly love to do. It's what you like to do to escape what you have to do.

What is it you'd really like to do?

Go back in your mind to when you were a child. We all had some vision of who we wanted to be as an adult.

What was the thing you loved?

Perhaps it was something you can no longer physically do. If that's the case, extend your view and see if something related is interesting to you.

For example, if you are a big sports nut but are not an athlete, maybe you can pursue another occupation in the sporting world. If you love watching sports, you might start a blog and eventually become a sports journalist. Do something that is connected to what you love to do.

Many people do actually make a living at what they love. I am a living, breathing example of this.

When I was ten years old I used to tell my mom that I needed to make a bunch of money by the time I was thirty so I could go pursue music. I lost sight of what I wanted to do over the years, and then I reclaimed it. Relatively late in life, I started having a music career.

Find what you love, and you can do it, too.

Pursue Your Dreams, No Matter Where They Lead You

I have been a musician at heart my entire life. I play twelve instruments and write songs, but I had a period where my talent laid dormant because I didn't have passion in my heart. I was pursuing money, and I was bored.

For ten years of my life, I hardly wrote at all. But since 2008, I have probably written almost five thousand songs. Most of my songs emanate from my love, my muse, good or bad. Sometimes I will pick a fight with her just to get a song, which I shouldn't admit, but it is the truth.

As I stated earlier, I have had the most improbable journey. Going from being a boring business owner to becoming an accomplished singer-songwriter and starring on a major TV Show is about as improbable as it gets. Eight years ago I was a regular old yuppie guy living a relatively typical life; that has all changed. Pursuing my dreams has led me to a life I love.

Don't Leave Any Opportunity Unexplored

I have never done anything in television before, but my willingness to explore this opportunity has given me an interesting new path. Opportunities present themselves all the time; you just have to recognize them and be brave enough to explore them.

My first business I started was when I was very young. I started an Information Technology (IT) business based on the Y2K scare—people were afraid the computer infrastructure would shut down when the year changed to 2000.

It sounded ridiculous to me, so I went to Borders Books and bought six different computer language books and learned the universal, simplistic things that had to be discovered in computer code to fix a calendar problem.

I designed a little scan tool. I don't recommend that you do this, but I applied for twenty credit cards on the same day. I pulled money off half the credit cards, did a balance transfer every month, and back then, you could get 1 percent back every time you did a balance transfer. My seed money was paid down by that 1 percent.

I soon became the main subcontractor for IBM for Y2K testing. Enormous companies relied on me. They had no clue that it was this kid who had a finance degree and knew nothing about computers had figured out this simple little thing.

That is one example of recognizing an opportunity when it was presented. The *One Shot* TV show, essentially a hip-hop *American Idol*, is another.

Week by week, we went to a different city and auditioned people to be the next big rap star. To each city, we brought a celebrity judge who was native to that city to guest judge with us. BET Network loved it; they picked up the show.

I knew nothing about television when we started this venture. We spent a ridiculous amount of money that I probably didn't have to spend, but I have no clue. We ended up having success.

The point I am getting at is that passion is not just pursuing the one singular thing that you love. Sometimes it's about giving other things a shot, and in doing so, you find out more about yourself. Don't turn away an opportunity just because you don't have experience in that particular field; you never know where it may lead you.

I have always been passionate about writing music and being an artist. Some people may not have that obvious a passion. If you feel like you don't have an obvious direction to head in, pursue opportunities in areas you have never explored before.

Get outside your comfort zone. The path that is being presented to you may lead to your passion. Opportunities are always presenting themselves; if you are paying attention, you will see them.

Always look at life as an *experience* as opposed to a *grind*. If you adopt that mindset, you will be amazed at what ends up happening for you.

CHAPTER FIVE

Balance

UNHAPPINESS COMES FROM EXTREMES

Unhappiness comes from extremes.

It's an age-old adage—Jesus said it, the Bible says it, pretty much every organized religion says it:

Everything in moderation.

Most people tend to get in trouble when they do too much of something. Too much of a good thing becomes a bad thing, like being a workaholic. You start out working hard toward a goal, and when it becomes so extreme that all you do is work, you leave out the other aspects of your life that are important.

What ends up happening is you lose focus of all the other things that you love, and this makes you unhappy.

How do you live in a manner in which you are in balance and you do things in moderation?

When you get off-kilter and go into an area where you're living very extreme toward one thing and have lost balance from all the other things that you love and need in your life, it leads to unhappiness. You have to develop tools in order to stay in that balance.

How to Maintain Balance Between Diet, Exercise, and Spirituality

In order to stay in balance, focus on the three components to your own physical and mental well-being:

1. Eating right
2. Exercising
3. Staying in balance emotionally

Like anything else, if you go too far in one aspect and neglect all the others, it takes you off balance.

If you focus too much on what you eat, don't exercise, and don't maintain a healthy mental lifestyle, it's going to throw you off-kilter.

The same thing will happen if you focus primarily on exercise and you don't care about what you eat or focus on your mental well-being. Similarly, you will be off balance if you focus only on your mental well-being and ignore your body.

In order to stay in balance, you have to make sure that you are allotting time for all three components of health. The way I do that is setting myself up on a schedule.

In a previous chapter, I talked about my diet and how important it is to set small goals that you will actually be able to adhere to. The same thing applies to exercise.

Look at your life in increments of a week at a time. Focusing on a year, five years, or ten years is completely overwhelming to me. Looking at life through weekly increments is how you are going to conquer any balance problems in life.

It may help to keep track of your goals in a journal.

Ask yourself this question each week:

In this week, what do I want to accomplish?

I always set one-week goals for my diet:

Okay, this week I'm going to have a cheat day Wednesday and a cheat day Sunday. The rest of the days I'm going to stay low-carb.

Same thing with exercise:

This week, I'm going to lift weights twice, run three times, and make sure I do my push-ups every day.

As far as emotional well-being is concerned, consider what helps you feel balanced. It might be meditation, yoga, music, art, or a hobby. Then, make a commitment to whatever you choose to do, keeping track of your plan in terms of hours or days that you are going to commit to that activity during your week.

For me, running is also part of keeping emotional balance, which makes it a two-in-one activity. It's something that I use to clear my head; it's a cathartic experience for me. For me, running is a kind of meditation.

Playing my guitar is another near-religious experience for me. In addition, I am taking care of my emotional well-being when I am writing my songs. The process of songwriting is very stream-of-consciousness, and I find it therapeutic. It is how I connect to my emotions.

I set aside time several days a week just to research and read different things that appeal to me as well. That includes reading books on economics, biographies, and also keeping up with current events.

How to Maintain Balance Between Your Life Partner, Your Children, and Your Work

In addition to maintaining balance between what you eat, how you exercise, and how you care for your mental well-being, it is important to balance your time between your life partner, your children, and your work.

When you are madly in love and you put all kinds of effort into your relationship, it's hard not to neglect the work or other loved ones. At home, you focus on your kids and lose sight of your work and your life partner from time to time. It can also be very easy to throw yourself into work and lose sight of your kids and your life partner.

This is the eternal struggle we all have. It is figuring out how to maintain a balance of the three that equal the Holy Grail of happiness in life.

How do I do it?

I live a life that is very compartmentalized. I make sure I set certain times every day to devote to work, to time alone with my life partner, and to times with my kids. I don't deviate from those times no matter what I have going on.

No matter how extreme it is, you have to accept that tomorrow is another day. Unless it is an absolute ring-the-bell emergency, you have to set times, almost with an alarm, for doing work, hanging out with your kids, and spending time with your life partner.

After a certain period, you will develop a rhythm that will become second nature. Generally, I spend two hours in the morning with my kids getting them off to school and helping my wife with all of the morning tasks. Then I will spend an hour with my wife in a private breakfast, and then I work for eight to ten hours. At night, I make sure that I have the two hours with the kids. Then they are in bed, so my wife and I have a couple of hours together before I do it all again the next day.

It is not easy. It also changes depending on your own needs for your career. As I am self-employed, I can run and lift weights during the day, so that doesn't impact my time with my wife and kids. You have to modify it as your schedule changes, but it is the key to happiness in life. You have to maintain a balance between all three; otherwise, you will never have true happiness.

How to Manage Your Week

When you look at your life, always look in terms of weeks. This strategy makes it easier to look at your calendars and make it all work. You can keep your weekly diet and exercise schedules and manage your work and play. You can allow for days when your work schedule is busy and note which days that you have off from work and can devote more time to your partner and kids.

Another important factor is your level of presence in your own life.

How present you are in your interactions?

Being present in your life means focusing attention on the moments you are living. We all know that you can spend hours on an activity while actually being absent.

Resist this temptation. It will add a great deal to the quality of your time with your loved ones and in your other interactions.

Be present in your life and stop looking for escapes.

Nowadays, most people look at the measure of success as having a lot of time to escape. That is not success; that's just escape. Most people have difficulty finding happiness and balance because they are escaping their lives by sitting around, taking a lot of leisure time, and distracting themselves from everyday life.

How can you find more time for what you want to do?

Look at your leisure activities to identify which ones are really escapes. The first one I found was TV. My way of avoiding life was popping on the TV and watching what was on. Now, I hardly watch television, and I am amazed at how much more time I have to pursue time with my life partner, do things with my kids, and work.

Minimize your leisure activities that aren't substantial — that are really just for killing time, and you will find more time for truly important activities in your week.

In addition, if you put proper focus on your health — diet, exercises, and emotional well-being — you will find that you actually have more energy that you can use in your week. All of these things are interconnected.

Look at your life with a critical eye and make sure you follow the previous chapters. You will find the energy, the yearning, and the ability to actually live life to its fullest. It will make you live with passion, recognize that each day is precious, and not waste a moment.

We have covered a variety of scheduling topics in this section.

To summarize:

- Keep everything in moderation as much as possible.

- Look at your life plan in terms of weeks, not months or years.

- Modify your schedule for special events or needs.

- Balance your time between your love partner, your children, and your work.

- Take care of your health with a regular plan; don't ignore any of the three elements—diet, exercise, and emotional well-being.

- Focus on your health—it will give you more energy and will increase the quality of your actions in all other areas.

- Be present in your life; don't escape.

- Look at your leisure activities and minimize the ones that are just for killing time.

- Live with passion.

Practice and you will develop a rhythm that will become second nature.

HOW TO LIVE EACH DAY IN BALANCE

In the previous section, I touched on several general topics related to living your life in balance from a weekly schedule. In this section, I will go in to a little more detail as to how I do this. In reading what works for me, you may find some tools that will help you to be able to achieve these measures yourself.

A Weekly Schedule in Detail

Like I said in the previous section, it is best to look at your life in terms of weeks. Don't look at it in months or years. Don't set unrealistic goals for yourself and then back off.

When you set yourself a schedule for a week, honestly look at the upcoming week that you have.

Is it an ordinary week in which you'll be following a regular schedule?

Are you traveling?

Do you have anything going on of monumental importance?

Make a weekly plan that incorporates your wellness schedule, your family, and any special needs.

For example, this week, I might figure out that based on what I have coming up, I can run on Tuesday and Thursday. My kids have a performance Wednesday night, and I am planning on going out with my life partner Tuesday night and grabbing dinner with her again Saturday night. We have some friends who want to come over and hang out.

Then I look at the whole week, and start making some decisions on what I *have* to do versus what I *want* to do.

Based on the above, my busy days at work are going to be Monday, Tuesday, and Thursday. So those are the days I probably shouldn't run, and if I am going to lift weights, I will do that toward the end of the day. Since my kids have special performances at night, I would counterbalance that with hanging out with my wife on a different night.

Look at the entire week as a whole. You may have to do a little juggling to make everything fit. Sometimes you have to choose to leave some things out.

Maybe this week I don't have time to spend with friends?

If this is so, I won't spend time with friends this week, but make a plan for another week. It's really important that you see other people that you love, and sometimes, if you want to do this, you may have to sacrifice time from another part of your life.

Look weekly at your entire life with a critical eye and with the understanding that your life partner, your kids, your work, and your passion are the four main parameters of life. Anything you want to do in addition to that has to fit in with those parameters.

Prioritize Each Day

I know that it sounds like I am a super-organized person. I am absolutely not.

Although I do plan my weeks, I wake up every morning and truly have no idea what exactly is going to happen that day. I don't ever wake up with much of a plan except the basic idea—like, I will know I am going to lift weights or run, and I might have something in mind about food. After I wake up I consider what I will do that day.

Do I need to work, or can I take the day and hang with my life partner or kids?

I try to set my mind as to what I would like to accomplish that day. It is not necessarily a list of tasks that I want to complete, but more so the mental goals that I would like to accomplish today.

What do I want to learn?

What experience do I want to get out of this day?

That is pretty much all the planning I do. I don't make detailed task lists; I let life take me where it's going to go on any given day.

Of course, every day is a little different. Sometimes you might wake up with a headache and are in a bad mood, and other times you wake up in a great mood. Your mind might be relaxed, or it might be more excited. Consider all of these things as you are brushing your teeth looking in the mirror.

I always ask myself: *What am I feeling today?*

What do I feel like focusing on?

Do I want to focus on something more emotional?

Am I feeling more like focusing on details that need organizing?

Do I want to work some deal today that I feel good about?

Where is my mindset today — where do I want to take myself?

Based on that, I engineer my day. Of course, things come at you that you don't have any control over, but you do have control over your own mindset. That is the ultimate filter as to how anything will seem on a given day.

If you are in a great mood, things are going to roll off your shoulders. If you wake up in a bad mood, it's going to filter how you see things.

If you feel like you are ready to take on the world, take on the world. But if it's one of those days where you want to stay under a blanket, make sure that you understand that this mindset is going to alter how you handle things on that day.

Be cognizant if your mindset doesn't match what is coming at you on any given day. Put it off until another day. This is what I mean by organizing your day; make sure that your day is in continuity with the mindset that you have when you start your day.

Try Not to Make Ironclad Plans

There is an old saying: If you want to make God laugh, tell him your plans.

None of us has a clue on any given day what is coming at us. It doesn't matter who you are; this is true for everyone. I woke up this morning having no idea what

I was going to be doing today, other than a conference call. The day has turned out completely different from what I expected it to be. That is great for me. I wake up every day not knowing what is going to happen.

The point is that I don't spend a lot of time trying to make plans because this is my life. My life is not very controlled, and I love it that way. I love the organized chaos in my life because it's what gives me the juice of living.

Don't make so many plans that you miss opportunities. Trying to control too many events in your life can cause you to go on a path that may lead you away from where you should be.

Wake up, make sure you are in tune with how you are feeling that day, and deal with things accordingly. If something comes at you that you don't like, set it aside. If you have things you have to do in a day, do them. But try not to set your days to such a schedule that you can't allow anything else in.

You want to leave room for a great opportunity to make its way to you; you don't want to crowd out all the unexpected, unique, and different experiences that might find you.

There is a lot you have to take on to live your life in balance. You have to coordinate everything related to your physical and mental well-being with your life partner, your children, and your work. You must organize all of that into daily and weekly schedules.

If you follow the steps that I've given you, not only are you going to be able to accomplish significantly more, but you are going to be extremely happy in your daily life. You will be able to give yourself permission to relax and realize that tomorrow is another day.

Do the most that you can for each task that day, and then accept that when time is up on that task, it's up. Don't feel bad about not completing things from time to time because you always have the next day.

THE NINETY-DAY ASSESSMENT: WHERE ARE YOU AND WHERE DO YOU WANT TO GO?

There is a reason why businesses often break things down into quarterly events. Ninety days is a good amount of time to look at where you have been, where you are going, and where you should be going.

Checking in quarterly to assess your own personal journey is a great idea.

Ninety days is the perfect time to give yourself an evaluation; it's enough time to see if what you are doing is working, and it is not so long that you will have assumed bad habits that will be hard to change.

However, there are many other benefits to doing this kind of assessment and we will discuss these in more detail:

- It sets you on a path that allows you to review what's happening on a regular basis.

- It allows you to take the time to recognize and celebrate your successes.

- It encourages you to assess your goals and improve them if needed.

- It helps you identify patterns that prevent you from succeeding.

- It is a mechanism for setting new goals and moving forward accordingly.

Create a Daily Email with the Same Subject Line

Every day I create an email with the subject line, "To Dos."

It's very simple. This series of emails has morphed into a daily journal of a sort. I list things I have to do, tasks I want to accomplish, what my mindset is, or how I feel about what I'm doing. Throughout the day, if I have the urge to, I will add things to it by creating another email.

If you do this, keep these emails archived and you will essentially be creating a journal for yourself. It's a good way for you to go back and look to see what tasks were pressing you ninety days prior.

Look back at your to-do emails every three months. You will get an idea of the arc of everything you have accomplished in that time, and how you felt along the way.

You will also see how wildly insignificant some things were over time. If you go back to look at the to-dos of a year ago you will read about the things that seemed so incredibly important to you then. It's going to blow your mind when you look at what you felt was so critical back then and compare it to where you are sitting today.

The point of doing this daily email is three-fold.

1. It will give you an important perspective. It will help you realize that there are things that may seem so overwhelmingly important at the moment, but in the long-term are not important at all.

2. It will give you an idea of how accomplished you truly are. You can look at all of these tasks you accomplished a year ago, six months ago, or three months ago and say: *Wow. I do a lot in my life*.

3. It gives you the ability to see what you are focusing on in your life. This is an important assessment to make. Look at what you are spending your time on and decide:

Do they matter?

If they do, that is fantastic. But if you are seeing a bunch of things that are mundane, unnecessary, or if you focused on things that don't really matter, it is time to reassess your priorities.

Start Each Quarter with What You're Trying to Accomplish

Every ninety days is a good time to assess:

- How much money did you make?

- Did you spend time with family?

- Did you do the things you wanted to do with your life partner?

- Have you kept fit?

- How did you feel physically?

Look at where you were, and then look at the next quarter of your life and figure out where you want to go from there.

Everything I try to do in life is accomplished via short, incremental planning. I don't believe in five-year or ten-year plans at all. When I think about where I was five years ago compared to where I am today, I couldn't even begin to tell you how I got from there to here.

If you had told me five years ago that I would have a hip-hop *American Idol* TV show and would be writing songs for some of the biggest performers on the planet, I would have said that you were out of your mind.

Five years ago, my new wife and I were about to have our baby together, and we had just merged all five other kids together. At the time, I didn't have a business because I had sold my business a year earlier.

Today, I have the TV show and am writing and performing constantly.

How would you even attempt to make a five-year plan that would encompass all of that?

You couldn't. It's ridiculous to even try.

I have found that results come most easily by breaking life down into bite-sized chunks, into small parameters so you actually have real tangible ability to succeed. You can set goals in ninety days for yourself and build upon those goals every ninety days. You may be shocked how much you can accomplish in ninety days.

To start, look at your life and say to yourself:

In the next ninety days, this is where I hope to be.

Stick to it. Do not take your eyes off the prize. Write it down.

At the end of the ninety days, did you accomplish it?

If you didn't, why didn't you?

You can try to accomplish them in the next ninety days. Or perhaps you might find that this goal wasn't the right fit. Assessing your life every ninety days will allow you to review the relevance of your goals as well as your level of progress toward them.

At the End of the Quarter, Review Your Goals

Part of the ninety-day period is assessing what you want to do, but also looking backward and recognizing that what mattered to you ninety days ago may have changed.

What matters to you today?

What are the impediments that prevented you from accomplishing it?

What do you need to look at differently to accomplish your goals?

You may find that you focus on the failure to complete the task as opposed to actually looking at it and trying to understand what caused hold-up.

You must think hard about the reasons:

Was it not meant to be?

Was it a bad idea?

Was something blocking your success?

Have a critical eye when you look at these setbacks but be sure that you are *analyzing what happened* instead of focusing on the failure.

Recall what you wanted to accomplish, go through your to-do emails for that previous ninety days, and figure out why you did not accomplish your goal.

The goals you *don't* reach give you important information. They can help inform you about certain things that might routinely block you from success. They can help you identify your bottlenecks — mental or physical hang-ups that prevent you from achieving your goals.

The whole reason for looking backward over a time period is to help you find patterns in your own life that prevent you from succeeding. Figure out how to go about correcting those bad patterns. Looking backward is the best way for you to go forward and achieve goals by correcting patterns that don't work for you.

When you are doing a ninety-day assessment, you will be looking at time broken down into daily, weekly, and quarterly tasks. You will be checking back to see what you have accomplished and then will make plans for the future.

If you look at life from those perspectives, you will be able to move ahead day by day, week by week, and year by year. You will be able to break patterns that have stood in your way for years. You may well be surprised at how much you are able to accomplish.

Conclusion

In 2008, I was:

- Overweight
- In a job that I was unhappy with
- In a marriage I was unhappy with
- Relatively disengaged from my kids

Now, eight years later:

- I am a TV star in a hip-hop reality TV contest show.

- I have become a country singer and songwriter working with the biggest artists on the planet.

- I am happily married to my college sweetheart.

- I have six children who I am fully engaged with and love every minute of every day I get to spend with them

If you put your mind to actually effecting change in your life, you can accomplish so much.

All of the elements that we covered in this book — physical and mental health; loving your life partner; parenting your children; pursuing your passions in life and in career; nutritional, physical, and mental well-being — everything comes back to just one idea:

Owning your life.

This means getting up every morning and not accepting a life of quiet desperation, but waking up and looking at yourself in the mirror and thinking:

I'm going to go out and accomplish all the things I want in my life today.

Don't be scared of living or of where life takes you.

Don't worry if life throws you a curveball. In fact, when you are trying to change your life, it makes sense to go with unusual or improbable opportunities, doesn't it?

Remember the old *Seinfeld* episode where George Costanza decided that the exact opposite of everything he has ever thought in life is right?

He started pursuing the exact opposite of what his original instincts were, and all of a sudden life started happening for him.

In a nutshell, it's like that. Shake off those bad habits and make purposeful changes.

Look at all of the things you tell yourself you can't do, and start doing them. Figure out what you really want to do with your life. Look at all of the things you wanted to do as a child and write a list. Think about what you most love to do. Don't worry about anyone thinking you're foolish and don't focus on money concerns. Start pursuing what you want.

Don't allow yourself to be overwhelmed with thoughts of impossibility.

I had no idea what the future had in store for me, but I stopped pretending that I did. When I stopped pretending that I knew what the future had in store for me, I decided to pursue my passion. All of a sudden, life took me on a whirlwind tour and took me to where I am today.

Be happy. Live passionately. Follow the guidelines in this book and take some cues from my past.

Then, just like me, you could actually be looking back at your life eight years from now saying to yourself:

Holy cow, I can't believe where I am today!

Next Steps

Please check out www.myoneshot.tv for more information about my TV show,

One Shot.

Please go to www.mikesmith.net to get your copy of my latest album, *Always You and Me*, with the chart-topping single, "Little Bit of Us," and win a chance to go to a live taping of *One Shot*, debuting August 23, 2016, on the BET Network.

About the Author

Mike Smith is a Cuban-American singer songwriter, musician, and businessman. Mike is a prolific songwriter. He writes an average of six songs per day and plays twelve musical instruments. He has written and recorded with some of the biggest artists in music including RZA from *Wu Tang Clan*, members of *Guns and Roses*, members of *Dave Matthews Band*, the seven-time Grammy-nominated *Avila Brothers, Tech N9ne, TI, Twista, Slaughterhouse*, and many others.

Mike stars in and is the Owner and Executive Producer of the reality competition show, *One Shot*, which debuts on BET in August 2016.

Additionally, Mike has owned and operated numerous businesses, including an IT Company and multiple chains of medical practices.

Mike was born in Philadelphia, grew up in New Jersey, and moved to North Carolina where he attended college. Mike currently lives between Charlotte, North Carolina, and Nashville, Tennessee, with his former college sweetheart, now wife, Erika Smith, and their six children.